ISBN No: 978-0-9561502-0-2

CONTENTS:

PAGE:

ALONE:

You and I were a work of art
A creative gift from the Creator's heart
In my eyes I saw you whole
The kind, loving completer of my soul

Placed upon the pedestal high
Our love for each other destined to die
Never did I think the fiery flame
As all the rest would go out the same

An ancient curse from an ancient crime
The revelation of a heart in time
Causing shifts in the sands of life
One by one the moments go by

Alone I wait the tears run dry
With no-one here to wipe my eye
Alone I think it's always the same
Forever, alone, I'll remain

A MOMENT IN ETERNITY:

Taken further
Sometimes ashamed
Who are we to judge?

Time and time again
We've seen
You accept regardless

But a precious moment
For a while shared
Gracious, taken
For hearts were bared

Recognise it's special
For another might not come
Once in eternity
Though keeping strength; young

Walk the way, this road is long
But you, arriving, know you're strong.

AN ANCIENT PAIN:

How can love, an ancient pain
This anguish in me cause again
When will I know it's just enough
When will I be placed above
The stranglehold of my own reflection
My Me, eternally facing rejection

APART:

I hate to be apart
It tears apart my heart
I don't know who I am
Without your guiding hand
You give me strength to face
Life in this dark place
I need you here with me
Love to set me free
Days without you near
Fill my heart with fear
From me never depart
I hate to be apart

BARED, BITTER CHILL:

Touched by your hurt
Compassion flowed
The crying heart
Through tears showed

I know your pain
I've felt your fear
I've seen God
As He draws near

God spoke to me
Showed me your heart
To make you at ease
Give you a start

For it seemed so bad
And probably was
You lived the pain
Then closed yourself

Because pain and guilt
Are bitter pills
They cause confusion
That knawing chill

Of knowing that to feel
Means losing control
Letting the dam-wall break
Releases your soul

How can you let go
You can't make it alone
The emotional flood
Of mistakes known

So I held you tightly
To show you I care
I'll keep you up
I'll always be there

  * So trust in God
  * And lay your heart bare.

BY YOUR SIDE:

I am just myself
I cannot be another me
Thrice taught, once rebelled
Founded, essence, in tranquillity

The strength of me lies in you
The 'other' held nearby
Gradually, sensing grew
Of feelings known as mine

My heart to yours replied
But another is by your side

CANDY-COATED WRAPPER:

—   For the question in the answer
    Remains the one you need
    My love restrained in passion
    Prepares the heart to grieve
    Like a candy-coated wrapper
    And the drawn out comfort zone
    Forever keeps the everlasting
    Days one calls one's own

Too many times before
I've seen this drama enfold
To lift me up and carry me on
To the repetitive slaves of old

Does one even bear the thought
To close your eyes and take the dive
When will it ever be enough
This stage of our lives

The day to day wondering
Of this the final cost
The leap of faith of every day
Will I find I've lost

 * And the jump of time
    Is the leap of faith
    Into nothingness
    Nothingness

CHAINS:

I wonder then, I wonder how
My past at work, my past here now
Twice as many, tombs of gold
Past the relics, names of old

To my side comes one in chains
From my heart, gone, remains
Where and when am I to be
Fondly tests insanity

One by one they all retreat
Facing giants they can't defeat
Is it not an ancient curse
This ritual pain we all rehearse

Take my hand, lift me up
Take this thorn, this crown, this cup
I am here with work to do
My job, my life, to die for you.

CHOSEN PATH:

Things come, things go
Waters rise, rivers flow
From in the earth a rich resource
Once broken, now in verse

A tiny bubble bursts through
Birthing life, waters new
How is it that ne'er we see
The glorious life, abundantly?

A fish swims past my feet
A nibble: returned my friendly greet
One by one the rocks are moved
As I wade through pools I choose.

CIRCLE OF LIFE:

Here I stand where confusion reigns
The ultimate test of my will
Do I stand or do I fall
Within me the fight rages still

Sometimes I wonder if this is my lot
Apart from the norms of my kind
Trying to conform but still remain me
How do I get out of my mind

  The circle of life is turning
  And I am stuck on the ride
  And I cannot see where I'm going
  Cause repetition has made me blind
  Am I moving forward or back
  Up or down or out
  Getting out of this dizzy turn
  Is what it's all about

I see the circle happen again
And again I want to cry
How can I be a child
As my life passes me by

I'm angry at me and the rest of the world
But they cannot understand why
I love and I cannot control it
No matter how hard I try

  The circle of life is turning
  And I am stuck on the ride
  And I cannot see where I'm going
  Cause repetition has made me blind
  Am I moving forward or back
  Up or down or out
  Getting out of this dizzy turn
  Is what it's all about

The circle is a given
Life and love and pain
Time after time I have to climb
This ladder once again.

COULD LOVE BE:

A new face draws my heart
After all these years of fear
Something in him tears me apart
In the gentle eyes appears

Not a lifetime, but many years
Something hidden in him remains
A troubled soul that just endures
Alone to bear his pain

Tender love, carefully shown
Could this be the way
Closer together, hearts grown
In beauty seen today

* Tell me one thing that fools can see:
  Is this possible; could love be?

CRUEL JOKE:

Always together when you are alone
Fate's cruel joke of icy water thrown
Everyone always loving and loved
But myself seeming always rejected and judged
By the being of me and the expression of mine
My life, my fate, always resigned

DEEP AND SHALLOW:

What is this life that within its depths
A heart of yearning grows
But if, once, tainted, broken
Never its true shelf shows

Childlike, open, to rejection's folly
The only time known
For after the fateful turning point
Past the child grown

How can one be who one really is
When the world cannot accept
So out of the hurt comes another person
Immune to this reject

  * The new one shallow, the old one deep
    This is how we ourselves keep

In simple language it means this:
As children we show ourselves completely
But after hurt, scorn and rejection
Only the shallow part can they see
The shadow of us which others cannot affect
Is all we will open to their reject

DEFINING WAY:

As a blood-red rose
My love bloomed

Now it's gone, who knows
Now it's doomed

As a bright, shining star
My passion burned

Now it's removed so far
From backs turned

As an ornate precious stone
My enthusiasm glowed

Now it's returned, alone
Slowly it slowed

They say: ignore what others say
But it always changes, hurts
In some defining way.

DOWNWARD SUCTION:

Another feel, a new hope
But turned soon upon its head
Give me freedom to resist
To stand within instead

Once it used to work for me
Shop, visit, read
Now there is nothing to pick me up
Nothing fills the need

One by one my passions fall
My heart tires of being alive
Floating, now, upside down
From death I can't revive

  * Pulled down, swept along
    Sad, tired, wrong.

DRIFTWOOD:

From an ancient time
Evolves the art of now
Seeming close, or far; sublime
Touches deep inside, somehow

Driftwood drifts, sea to shore
To tell nature's story
Once again, as seen before
The life, in deathly glory

Minutes and years etched alive
Wondrously, it travelled far
To wash up here, to remind
Resounding, as on a guitar:

Remember, always, in all your ways
The everlasting
Ancient of Days.

EBBING LIFE:

The lost can find and the blind can see
But the weight of the world
Can't be lifted from me

For my life of hope is now a life of pain
And the cycle of hell
Starts around again

Exhaustion strips what life was here
From inner self
Rises only fear

One by one my resources fail
Left behind
A ghostly trail

To leave me here, the world moves on
Alone I remain
Ebbing life gone.

EBBING SEA:

Suddenly, the weight of the world crashes over me in one gigantic wave. I can't breathe – the weight and darkness press all around me, whilst bitter salt water fills my lungs.

I sink, lower, weighted down, into the cold, wet sand I'm buried, like a small, insignificant sea crab. Lower and lower, further and further from the light I sink, and despair envelops me, my thoughts, my mind, my life.

In total darkness I wait, for someone to rescue me.

My heart can no longer contain this weight. Will it be lifted, or will I sink into oblivion and become part of the ebbing sea?

ECHOES:

Fallen slowly, like leaves to the ground
The impact hard, does not resound
Echoes of my heart's own pain
Reverberate softly through me again
Unnoticed strain seeps through my mind
Knife sharp shards pierce and blind
Outer illness the body shows
Inner destruction no-one knows

ENOUGH:

Tear me down, cut me up
Cast me away like an old plastic cup
Take my heart and stop it beating somehow
'Cause nothing could be worse than the pain I feel now

ENTIRELY MINE:

The ocean roared my heart's dismay
When I heard my friend you'd passed away
The seagulls cried my screams of pain
When I thought I'd never see you again
The thunder crashed with my anger's rage
When I felt forever had turned your page
But know my friend that all the time
The ache and tears are entirely mine

ERRING ON ME:

My name and my place, the hope of my days
What does myself mean to me?
Strength and love divided and flows free, yet restricted
The time of erring reflected in me
Scrutinised, taken apart, rejected
The course of my life forever determined
Who I may be and where I may stand
By hateful, spiteful people who don't understand

FATE REVERSED:

I saw your hurt plainly through the words
The frustration and desperation, perturbed
Feeling lost, lonely, alone
Can fate not be turned?

I cried in empathy, your pain and mine
One who shared my feeling of being left behind
Grafting my way; two forward, one back
You to remind

Now here I stand changed, in your role
I wonder how you did it, how you became whole
You're gone now, leaving me alone
To the completer of your soul

   * And I am empty
    I try to fill your shoes
    But I don't know how
    I can't be you
    I need your loving arms to pull me through.

FLAME:

Torn apart, across, my heart
Being once, being me
Further grown in jaws alone
Wondering what is free

Falling fast, without grasp
Down again below
Failing mine, one at a time
My life, me, slows

Gratings closed, juxtaposed
Life, alive, live
Laws of life within my mind
Dictate: always give

* The candle's flame
  Seems the same
  Then instantly flickers out.

FOUNDATION:

A shifting course, a path unknown
Taken before the way itself shown
Many ways too intense to behold
A life of lies in one breath told

Step by step a different me
Emerges together, for all to see
Myself hidden through clouds of lies
Woven to protect from prying eyes

At each turn mistakes made
A heart ripped in two displayed
The part that no-one wants to see
Broken, shouldered, deep within me

Too many changes, so much loss
Each new bridge another cost
Foundations rocked and I'm forced along
A shifting course down a path unknown.

FREEDOM FIGHT:

A poster gleams, it shouts to me
More embittered, more obscure
A dance; work; a new face
Things flash past me in a blur

A freedom fought, a battle lost
Exhausted, spent, dead
A life unworthy, trials met
I scream, it churns instead

Graphics sharp, yellow on black
Retreating, backwashed tide
The wholeness of the deep green sea
Engulfs me as I hide

Two wonders here, a soft sigh
Clambering for the shore
I bob up and down as I try to breathe
Returning, lost, for more

The drab, dark grey of an endless night
Turns laughs into powerful fear
Time spent alone drives me deeper down
Past ancient faces that appear

A gross encounter of a numbered kind
Panic subsides, replaced with loss
The grief of a child compares to none
Except a rolling, stoneless moss

Death is not all that causes grief
My question; the answer known
For I have seen its other side
My loss, grief has shown

The flight of an eagle touches me
As it soars on winds of change
But me I stand, rooted here
Freedomless, I remain.

GIANT'S LEAP:

Once more your face appears
As I struggle to focus through my tears
All I want to do is cry

Confusion mixed with fear
In this time I so need you near
I don't understand why

You promised to always care
No matter what you'd always be there
Where are you now?

And so I must repair
Shattered, stripped, my heart is bare
The pain you allowed

Your love and strength no more known
In fear I stand here alone
Alone before a giant's leap
The heart you were meant to keep.

GOLD DARKNESS:

Light is darkness
For the sun and the moon
Shine as grey as the day
Though the sky is blue, I'm told

My heart is heavy
For its cry is of longing
And emptiness remains
Too painful: the thought of you, to behold

My spirit is oppressed
For I, me; rejected
The shadow of my life; today
Hidden arms are few: to hold

Hence the light is darkness
And my passions empty gold
For others' hearts are cold.

GONE:

I wanna go home
I wanna go back
To the time of innocence
Of painless lack

Is it better to have loved and lost
Is it a punishment to count the cost

Now is forever
And I want to die
You walked out on me
Without even a goodbye

GUILT:

The heavens dark, the ocean deep
In our minds our lives we keep
For when our souls wander deserted plains
Our hearts and thoughts on mistakes remain

   The little one said: is it always true
   That one step at a time my Me becomes You?

The past, the future, our lives entwine
Forever encompassed by the sands of time
Always night, awake or asleep
The heavens dark, the ocean deep

HELL'S DARKNESS:

Why does the light rarely touch within
Why does the darkness always return?
The clouds descend over wasted heart
And the fire quickly dims

Spiralling downward every day
Taken further from the light
No hope in this cold, dark place
Life seeping away

It seems the punishment for every sin
Weighted on one mind
This hell's darkness surrounds again
The light never touches within.

HELL'S GRATE:

Angels of mercy carried me
Through all the years of pain
Exhausted, stripped, nothing left
Beaten time and again

One by one people fail
Lives pass on by
No-one truly wants to care
Why storms rage inside

The deep, dark pit of hell
Before me lies in wait
To strike down three crowns
Leaving me to cruel fate:

* my love, hope and faith
  cast into hell's grate

HERE ALONE:

Seeing the past, my life entails
When at last will I be free?
Through the pain and blinding tears
Emerge parts of me

Lost and blind I stumble on
Through the wilderness of my mind
Many times, too much to take
Life leaves me behind

The terrors of my nights, the fears of my life
The dangers still unknown
Throughout all, this day, this life
I know I'm here alone.

HE SUFFERED TOO:

A terrified child hides under the bed
Trying to escape the shame
His father does things he doesn't understand
The cycle repeated again
And he trembles in fear and silently prays
Lord, please let it end
Lost in the torment and the shame
In his life darkness descends

* For all those who've lost their hope
  Who suffer in silence each day
  Torment and fear their only friends
  As life slowly ebbs away
  No-one could ever truly know
  The pain that you've been through
  Except for Jesus, for He was a man
  And He suffered too

A young lady's life destroyed in one day
Through the choices of one man
Her self and her joy replaced by fear
That no-one can understand
And daily she struggles, desperate and alone
No-one knows her pain
She feels forever trapped by the fear
That envelops her time and again

- As the lashes tore pieces of flesh from His body
  As the nails pierced His hands
  And the blood poured down from that cross, for you
  I know
  Jesus understands.

HOPE:

A rare moment of clarity: a gift, as a day without pain. A flash of how my life once was, before the confusion, before the veil, before the guilt. A tentative hope my eyes might see – one day. As energy once surged through me, sparking excitement, exhilaration, a feeling of invincibility; so too does this one moment lift me out of the dark sameness of this my current existence. Just for a moment I glimpse with clear eyes what could have been. What might be. As the veil is lifted over foggy landscapes after nature's washing, my head rises just above the rim, just over the top, just long enough to see one bright colour.

HOW:

How can I love you
When you are not here
How can I show you
That you are dear

How can I be sure that
Our love will last
Through all the years as
Time goes past

When you were here
Our love was strong
Though all the time you felt
Something was wrong

In-between all the
Times we shared
I really tried to show you
That I cared

How is it, then, that
Now you're gone
Where is the love
Never-ending and strong

How come you promised to
Always be there
Now you're gone -
Do you still care

How come is love always
So far away
When will it be mine and
When will it stay

How can one's journey
Be always alone
And why does my love
Turn hearts to stone

* Why are you far when I need you near
  How can I love you when you are not here?

HOW IT IS NOW:

Suddenly, deep within me
Pain strikes its resounding gong
And I try, I try so hard
To be myself and to remain strong

But everything hurts
I don't understand why
What is wrong? I wonder
As I try not to cry

I feel out, I feel misled
But more than all confused
Where am I going and what have I done
How many have I used?

I wish I could start afresh
And be a better me
Then maybe I'd feel more whole
With more dignity

But when and where does change begin
And do I really care?
It may sound harsh - I suppose it is
Still, I must be fair

It seems my heart doesn't fit
Where can I empty it out?
How much longer must I sit and wait
With pain and endless doubt?

Take me away from this world I despise
For I am the cause of my true love's demise

I want to scream and yell and cry
What's the matter with me?
Is there no-one, no place at all
That someone needs me be?

Cold and alone, scared and confused
My life can't be as bad as it seems
But one way or another something must give
To release me into liberty

HOW MUCH:

* Heaven cannot contain
  hell cannot describe
  the power of emotion
  that rages deep inside

How much can one person take
How much can one person face alone
Before the end, before the heart
Explodes or turns to stone

When should one stop trusting
In those who say they'll never
Hurt you, leave you or reject you
From now until forever

What is my life but days on end
When I look for other ways to pretend
That all is well and I'm okay
How can I continue living this way?

IDENTITY:

Once dedicated always cruel laments
Of what was or should have been
The "subtlety" of people's beliefs and views
Released in words and anxious screams

A lifetime of hopes and dreams relent
Under the pressure of others' views
Buried beneath the weighted smiles of
This life we're forced to choose

  * Identity built or born dismayed
    The long, lifetime struggle displayed

IN LOVE'S WAY:

As I watched beyond the shadow of me
There came a breeze silently
For once in a lifetime an angel appears
Swiftly bearing away tears

To venture out and lose is gain
But never without its untimely pain
When will the light of a shadowy me
Burn brightly for eternity?

Knowing the cycle of daunting rejection
Does the decision even bear reflection?
Sometimes purposefully, sometimes not
Always the same; always another shot

For the life-strings of our purposed lives
Within and around each other entwines
So this the ultimate, age-old question;
A lover's heart in a bound confession:

Do I place myself in love's way?

IN THE NIGHT *(transl.)*:

I wake with a fright, peaceless
The devil and his helpers
Force my soul and spirit apart

Reality and dream, in and within each other
The whole night, through everything
I know they're there

From the distances of my guilt and the depths of my hurt
Doubt and a nauseous feeling
Ring their familiar bells again

  My restless soul begins to calm down
  I open my eyes
  I see my life in danger
  The entire me exposed

Something glorious, singing, at the foot of my bed
My own wonderful angel
Here to save me

She creates a peace within me and calmly I sleep again.

I STAY:

We met up as strangers
And later became friends
How come the good in life
Always fades, always ends

You lifted me up when I was falling
And carried me with your strength
You always turned when you heard me calling
With no thought to resent

The unfairness of our race against time
Hurts me more every day
The sharing of your life with mine
Ends in a tragic way

For such a short space
We shared our hearts
And now God has placed
Us on different paths

I wish I had more time to say
All the things in my heart
But you go
I stay.

JOYS OF BEAUTY:

A rose, without you, doesn't smell sweet
A robin's song, without you, incomplete
The powerful ocean, without you, is weak
The majestic mountains, without you, bleak
A tropical rainforest or a shooting star
Without you remain: remote, afar
For none of the joys of beauty do I see
When you are not here to enjoy them with me.

JUST ONE WORD:

Just one word can mean so much
Just one smile, just one touch
My river of pain flows so strong
With just one shout or just one wrong
Can't you see that I hurt too
Deep inside, deeper than you

Many times I've cried
When I've seen or when I've heard
The love that's close behind
Following just one kind word

Just one word can shatter my wall
Lift me up when I fall
Or like a dagger in my soul
Just one word can leave a hole
A never-ending well of pain
Made deeper again and again

Many times I've cried
When I've seen or when I've heard
The love that's close behind
Following just one kind word

Just one word can lift me high
Send me soaring through the sky
Or just one word can knock me down
And leave me there to be found
Can't you see the power behind
Words of love or words unkind

Many times I've cried
When I've seen or when I've heard
The love that's close behind
Following just one kind word.

KAITLYN:

The inspiration for a family's love
Grace was poured out from above
A miracle from God's own hand
Powerful love we cannot understand

You were created to be the best
Your life, love and talents blessed
One thing will always see us through
The knowledge that we are blessed with you

You introduced us with big blue eyes
And a smile that unlocked the greatest prize
Of knowing treasures forevermore
The day this miracle knocked at our door.

LIFE:

Sometimes ten minutes can seem like forever
Yet sometimes a day is not enough
Like when you're waiting in anticipation
Or when the sun sets on an old friend's visit

Sometimes life seems full of joy and happiness
Yet sometimes filled with pain and grief
Like when in love you're on top of the world
Or when rejection's slap turns you away

Sometimes life can seem unfair
Yet sometimes grace abounds
Like when failure comes despite all your efforts
Or when you soar to success on miracle's wings

Sometimes you're in a 25-hour, 8-day hurry
Yet sometimes you have all the time in the world
Like when tests and deadlines mean you can't stop to see
Or when a flower in bloom makes you sing and shout

Sometimes no restful sleep will come
Yet sometimes sublime peace reigns
Like when you wake up all the time or you toss and turn
Or when it seems as if angels guard your sleep

Sometimes life brings out the best in one
Yet sometimes seems to relish in disgracing you
Like when you rush to offer help, rescue, advice
Or when cowardice afforded, you close your eyes or turn your back

Sometimes you think you'll never be happy
Yet sometimes you've never been happier
Like when your efforts at human warmth return unrequited
Or when what you feel in you heart is mirrored by another

Life is the hardest journey of all
Discovering that you're on it alone is the hardest realisation of all
Still continuing despite all of this is the most courageous act of all

LITTLE HURT BIRD:

Treated with a living shoulder
Found my place but not in choice
Is it right to keep my place
Whilst within me the rage of noise

I am not a child of joy
But still my heart a factory line
Producing from within a crop
The life and steps, tendered, mine

Given, prescribed, I wonder how
People find their way alone
Teach me, lead me on my way
My path, my job, but not my own

Growing pains, temporally bound
How can it be this way but not
A rollercoaster prison ride
Mistakes and hurts no-one forgot

I am but a grounded bird
Wounded, failed, alive
When I feel winds try to lift
My spirits, me, revive

    * I fly, fall, cry.

LOSS BURNED:

The spiral drags me down
As the pain draws me in
Memories of my life with you
Return to me again

Falling through the sand
Sleeping as awake
Shadows the only sign of life
That light from darkness breaks

You were once my all
Before this pit of hell returned
Into the night you took my heart
And forever loss burned.

LOST:

I watch the blood spill from my arm
As the tears spill from my eyes
I wait for the warning, the silent alarm
But it doesn't; no one hears my cries

The light tower burns from a faraway place
But it doesn't guide my way
My mind throws me through time and space
The end light years away

When does the hurt ever begin to fade
When will the terror subside?
From now until the end displayed
My answer: silence replied

LOVE:

Love is like an ocean's roar
A powerful drawing to the shore
Yet love is like a gentle stream
Flowing, softly, towards a dream

Love is like an eagle's wings
A soaring, lifting, heart that sings
Yet love is like a robin's breast
Quietly offering its best

Love can be a raging storm
Tearing, destroying, causing mourn
Yet love can also be the day
When sun shines and lights the way

Love can be a bitter pill
Taken once, causes chill
Yet love can be a costly potion
That causes precious life devotion

Yet all these words can not describe
Not nearly what I feel inside
Tasting your love, seeing your heart
I never want to be apart

You, receiver of a tortured soul
Prepared for all to make me whole
For in the awakening of hearts bared
Lies the realisation of an eternity shared.

LOVE DIVINE:

You touched my soul
You reached my heart
Walls once of stone
Broke apart

Your caring arms
Exposed a part of me
Vulnerable tears
That no-one sees

Tenderly touched
Your hand in mine
Just one taste
Of love divine

ME INSANE:

As the time of life ticks by
The sands of my story trickle away
And the grating course refined
Cracks and scars left on display

Turning the weight in my mind
I see the reflection shimmer and fade
Myself as one leading the blind
My thoughts further astray

Formed and scarred by the arrows of others' piercing pain
Though without them never known: self or me insane.

MEMORIES' SHORE:

A far away place on memories' shore
A light, in the distance of time
Comes one to me, as many before
With a heart on a platter: for mine

Rejoicing, light-hearted steps
Towards another downward jail
Faces of old the ocean reflects
Mournfully gone with a whale's tail

  * Sands as memories, time, energy
    Quickly come, many, gone

Bejewelled, sparkling, passionate shell
Too much as always, I know
From the heights of love to rejection's hell
And I watch another one go.

MOMENT IN ETERNITY:

Taken further
Sometimes ashamed
Who are we to judge?

Time and time again
We've seen
You accept regardless

But a precious moment
For a while shared
Gracious, taken
For hearts were bared

Recognise it's special
For another might not come
Once in eternity
Though keeping strength; young

Walk the way, this road is long
But you, arriving, know you're strong.

MONSTERS:

Emotions from my anxious fears
Arise to drive me towards my tears
That well up whenever no-one sees
The hurting, inside, real me

Too much thought and too much pain
The senseless ideas rise again
How to make the hurt subside
Turn the focused thoughts aside

One by one I watch them appear
With an almost surprising, painful sear
The drops of blood rolling off my arm
Must surely help. They do not calm

The real me, what's inside
Becomes at times too much to hide
Fighting through another day
Just to keep these monsters at bay.

MY HEART:

I see my heart before me lying crumpled on the ground
And I look to see if there is any comfort to be found
But it seems that no-one notices that I am on my own
And no-one seems to care that I am scared and I'm alone

So I walk up to my heart, pick it up off the floor
And I try to put it back in its place as it was before
But it doesn't seem to fit, it's been disfigured from the pain
So I have to start reshaping and rebuilding once again

As I sit here in my bedroom, trying not to cry
I don't hear your footsteps as you're quietly walking by
But you stop and turn around and silently come in
And I don't hear you thinking that you've been where I've been

You can see what I'm thinking and you know that I have tried
You can see I'm feeling helpless and time's not on my side
So with compassion you walk to me and look me in the eye
But something there freezes the words you have inside

You have seen the look before you - in your very own eyes
When you felt all alone and no-one heard your heart's cries
All you wanted back then was for someone to be there
To hold you and to love you and to show you that they care

Instinct kicks in you realise words are not enough
Looking at your face I realise what I see is love
My heart is strangely tugged at but I don't know what to say
And I'm crying as you hold me and tell my it's okay

You and I both know the scars never totally heal
For the memories are there to remind us that it's real
But I cannot deny the change you've brought in me
I'm ready to become the best that I can be

Selflessly you cared for me and held me when I cried
And I cannot forget about you even if I tried
But being apart is causing my heart to tear in two
What can I say other than I really miss you

Once or twice you showed me a side I'd never seen
And I felt that I was treading where no-one had ever been

I want to show you that your fears are not your own
For I am here to share them and you are never alone

I don't know why this happened - it seems kind of strange
But I do know that I love you and that will never change
I feel like I'm dying - it's rough to be apart
But no matter where we are

You're always right here in my heart.

MY ME:

Hounded by eternity
Thoughts of my own heart
To me
You
Follows through
Trials that tear apart

Given once, thought I knew
Where and who am I
Here now
Apart somehow
Grounded, here I lie

One by one they pass me by
Strong and on their own
I try to stand
Take my hand
Fallen, I'm alone

Eagles fly effortlessly
I long for wind to soar
But I remain
Still the same
Taken as before

* My ME: changed, ignored.

MY TROPICAL EXPLANATION:

The tropical rainforest of my life
In an instant turned to grey
The day I heard from you the truth
Its safety ebbed away
From far across a chasm wide
I saw you watching me
It remained between us though I tried
To cross eternity

Instantly from child to adult, the truck developed me
Experienced then and many more, living fearfully

Somehow the colours of my life managed to shine through
Though I had to be a double me
A silver-birch for you

A grey depression fills my soul as my world comes crashing down
I try naively to hold on to some as pieces fly around

Suicide waves its darkest clouds; I readily give in
I wake to find myself still here, not in sweet oblivion

Existing, walking, I long for the past
When all was simple I was free
Now emotions rule my life, and govern who I must be

The silver from a tall, deep birch who talked and made me feel
Consciously, dead inside - you're gone; is this real?

Leaving loss, my cycle starts
I walk as if in a dream
This isn't real, it can't be true
"Come back to me!" I scream

You recognise it all in me, it's all too familiar too
You hold me close and see me stripped
"Hold on 'till you're renewed"

Bit by bit I start to grow, leaves start to sprout
With genuine joy and your branch in mine
I start to peel off the doubt

Only once this tree stands free
Tall and evergreen
Will I find my place in my tropical rainforest
Seeing what I've never seen

It's what I want - Evergreen - tall and sure of me
Not a birch or conifer
Interdependent
Free.

NEVER:

It was the chance of a lifetime
A dream come true
The day I realised
My love for you

Even better
Life became
When you confessed
Your love the same

Never have I
Been hurt that much
Never have I
Felt so out of touch

For when you walked out
Without looking back
You took my life
All that I had

I never ever
Want to see your face
Never again
Will I take your place

Never again
Will you find my voice
My help, my love
Taking back your choice

Live your life
I hope it's good
And always know
I NEVER understood.

NONE LIKE YOU:

Hold my hand, Father
Show me the way
Help me stand
And face the world today
You are my all
My mercy, strength and grace
Father hear my call
Let me see Your face
I worship You in all I do
For Lord, there is none like You

OBSCURE:

How can life be so obscure
To the littlest ones with hearts so pure
When will the cycle of innocence lost
Perpetuated beyond all cost
Be found to stop. When will we care
Enough to show our anger where
One of supposed wisdom and age
Grips little ones in terror's cage
What are we doing to keep them pure
Little ones with lives obscure

OCEAN'S REGRET:

The Ocean majestic, the sea pure
As eternal as the sky
Together forever, safely sure
On eagles' wings we fly

A cyclic force, a weight thrown
Drawing waves to shore
The tearing pressure of hearts known
As on rocks before

Ancient cries of sea-bound pain
Return as guiding lights
Drawn, thwarted, to never again
Sail the sea by night

The wondrous power of a perfect thing
Far beyond the mind
Meant to be, yet everything
Curses what we find

How can it be so blind?

ONE HARSH WORD:

Gone is the light and gone is my day
Taking from me forever this day
My feelings of love, peace disturbed
Forever destroyed by one harsh word.

PASSIONATE FRIEND:

From an impossible night
A never-again stance
Came an overpowering light
And a knowing glance

Once before I saw it there
The same feelings known
Yet, that time, not shared
A one-way, cold stone

But you knew me
And you felt me
Shared my pain
Felt it again
Held me tight
Made it alright

You and I
In a dream to last
Lifting us up
Together, the past
Is nothing and none
For by your side
My life has begun
Hope's revived

THEN...

In the darkness of hell
Painful words spoke
To bid farewell
From the dream awoke

To never again
Be where I belong
Passionate friend
You're forever gone.

PLEASE SEE ME:

You look at me
But you don't see me
You listen to me
Yet you don't hear me

I stand beside you
But you're far away
My heart tremors
Yet you don't feel me

The sands of my time
Drain beside you
But you don't notice
And you don't catch me

I pour myself out
But you don't care
You don't even realise
When I'm not there.

POISE:

My eye is caught by a piercing gaze
A sleek body poised to raise
Pointing up towards that magic lock
That intrepid explorers from adventure blocks

Once freed, adrenaline flows
Gleeful abandon in that body grows
Racing outside, into unnoticed rain
Stopping short, your consternation plain

Quickly thinking, purposefully you sit
To all to scratch a non-existent itch
Then with a swishing tail and a flicking head
Poise restored, loftily off you tread.

PRETENCE:

Familiar place, seen before
Heart gripped in terror's claws
Shock and sadness seem to be
The eternal path set out for me

Mistakes seen through visioned lens
Holy water cannot cleanse
Guilty crosses rise up this day
Mercy's branches fade away

Darkness breaks over my head
Releasing fears, that anxious dread
Too much time, too much pain
Night-time terrors rise again

Thus my body broken down
Soul and spirit start to drown
Self that's left I try to sense
Nothing escapes from this pretence.

REJECTION'S REGRESSION:

One by one people come
Meet, learn, know
To take my heart, a friendship start
Then break it, reject, go

To leave it there isn't fair
I play a role too
I try to be true to me
But I'm too much for you

The moon draws waves to shores
As I am drawn to them
But full of fear, afraid to be near
They turn and leave again

What's in me that people see
That makes them change their minds?
When all I can is what I am
Or is it me that's blind?

Receive, reject, unkind.

REPLACED BY LIFE:

Earthly bound, the laws of life
Dictate how much I may love you
Only to here, only in this way
For normality revolves around two

When we met we were one and one
Both hurting and singularly alone
Reaching out towards each other
To a friendship both could call their own

But life is hard and usually unfair
As we'd both discovered before
So, solace found in shared experience
Understanding exploded through love's door

You were the first to not reject
And always understand
You loved regardless, and kept alive
Hope; as you took me by the hand

Never in my life was anything unconditional
Before your faith, love and care
Amidst the many things you said
You promised to always be there

Drawn, magnetised, iron to iron
As one man sharpens another
I held on to the only safe thing
Your love became my cover

Closer together, circumstances aside
I thought we were deeper involved
But though you loved me, your feelings differed
"In motivation," though, "not depth," you told

Forever together, bound by love
A friendship to withstand time and space
So I thought, and I really believed it
Now another's taken my place

It hurts even to see your face.

SCRUTINY:

Crucial terminality to yourself and your own reward
Life plays games to determine how you hold up under scrutiny
If you don't pass the test of approval "normality" as a label fails
Sometimes you can make it there, against yourself
Sometimes not. Just having to survive
Eventually you mould.

SECOND CHANCE:

One chance is all you'll get
People may change but your course is set
After my one love walked away
I never thought I'd hear another one say
Words of love and hope to me
Enveloping love that sets me free
Touch me with your hand, your heart
My love, I never want to be apart
Your touch, your kiss, your loving glance
You'll always be
My second chance

SHORES OF JERICHO:

Waves come and waves go
Upon the shores of Jericho
My walls, my home, my life all gone
What once seemed right now wrong

Tiny birds come to me
They touch my heart, make me see
Life is but a cyclic force
Binding us to stay its course

Whosoever learns my name
Hears my heart, feels the same
Given once it calls no more
Beating waves upon its shore

For I am not indestructible
Iron to iron defensible
The grating of a painful mind
Causes blindness of a different kind

I stand alone upon this shore
The waves stiller than before
Never-ending time returns
To whisper, forever, sacred yearns.

SO FAR AWAY:

I see your face before me
A small faraway picture
Yet you haunt me every second of every day

You're in my heart, in my mind
In my thoughts that keep me blind

You're in the smell of a passer-by
The essential, permeating cry

You're in the bird who made his home
In the room you called your own

You're in a dog, a fluffy toy
That once you brought to bring me joy

You're in a song, one we shared
That played when first my love I declared

You're in the rain that now falls so much
The walks with which we shared its touch

You're in the memories of times together
The place I want to stay forever

You're in a certain special place
Where only OUR shadows graced

You're in my bed as I remember too
The way you'd draw me close to you

You're in the pain only you and I know
That brought us close to love and grow

You're in the touch I still remember
And the pain of a missed fourteenth of December

You're in my heart, and there to stay
But... my heart, my love
You're so far away.

SOMEONE CARES:

When cold winds blow
And darkness descends
When my arms are weak
And I can no longer pretend
My thought return to
Times we've shared
And my heart rests
In knowing someone cares.

STRUCK DOWN (AGAIN):

Up and down, a rollercoaster ride
One day the floor, the next the sky
Never calm, thrown about
With rough emotions casting doubt

I'm not at rest, I can't be whole
For with vicious claws you grip my soul
The demon-life of circular pain
Depression strikes me down again

THAT WAY:

A misunderstanding clear as day
I never intended it this way
We see these things so differently
With hindsight, retrospectively

One by one, events occurred
Yet, communications we misheard
Causing us to blindly go
Without establishing what we know

You don't know me or how I share
Love and trust for whom I care
The way I speak, the way I act
Shows only me, and that's a fact

I guess I thought you understood
That through all and over time we could
Remain trusting, caring, as friends should stay
But I guess you didn't see it that way.

THE BATTLEFIELD:

Battles fought, wars raged
All the time hearts caged
Friendly faces nowhere seen
Seems that's where I've always been

Pin-prick pain of one harsh word
More damage does than limbs disturbed
Though the pain seems not quite real
Inner scars that never heal

When one loves is love not true
How, then, can I help love you?
Your vow to never let the friendship end
From one to another dearly loved friend

I owe so much to you, you see
For when you loved you set me free
Now your heart towards me revealed
I lie, struck down, on this battlefield

You pull it out, then wipe its blade on the grass.

THE DAGGER IN MY HEART:

The dagger in my heart
As a thorn in my side
You, me, apart
Nothing, though I tried

Promises, vows
Made lovingly in truth
So tell me, then, how
Can you do what you do?

How can you take away
The one thing that made sense
Now all that remains
Is me from this day hence

Love deepened from a restart
But your love for me has died
The dagger in my heart
As a thorn in my side.

THE DAY I RAN (THE FROG'S TESTIMONY):

And I wander alone
Past a frog on a stone
For me life began
Not in birth
Or one day in church
For me: the day I ran

The frog blinked at me
Hopped on to a leaf
Leaving me all alone
After what I'd been through
No idea what to do
Left to survive on my own

One man in the fields
Adulthood reveals
Yet I didn't know it then
Forever affected
Feeling rejected
Started before I was ten

So the frog has to stay
As I run away
From confusions I don't understand
To home I can't go
So they'll never know
Of that day in the fields on the sand

I wonder: why me?
Did it just have to be
Or did I do something wrong
Should I have taken more care
Or not have been there
Try to resist, though he was strong?

The memories that scar
Persist, hurt and mar
Forever now part of me
My frog on a tray
Someone dissected today
That day; his testimony.

THE DEATH OF FOREVER:

I thought I had loved
I thought I knew
But I hadn't met love
'Till I met you

You lifted me up
Gave me wings to fly
I soared on your strength
As the days went by

Never had anyone
Loved me like you
I thought it would last
I thought it was true

Then in an instant
Everything changed
Someone found out
Someone forbade

And you listened to them
Left me hanging dry
All your promises of together
Forever, just died.

THE DUST BENEATH MY FEET:

I feel the dust beneath my feet
As I flail along the path
It seems to be a certain defeat
Those irons of my past

I wake from the journey of peaceless sleep
To an endless, drawn out day
Life at times can seem so cheap
To those who don't have to pay

For the nightmare of life is always at play
And I am forced to fight
Forever the cold dawn of day
Haunts my costly flight

I reach for something calmly sure
Always just out of reach
Those I grasp cannot endure
And fade as the dust beneath my feet

    ** If my weighted past remains behind
      What is left to reflect this mind?

THE EFFECTS OF COMMON HURT:

Thoughts shared, hearts bared
You and I as one
Changed forever, still together
Closer we become

How I tried through tears I cried
To show a deeper me
It's harder now, strange somehow
For our friendship just to be

Though things have changed, our love remains
Deeper than before
For I could show and now you know
The life at my core

But it seems to me, retrospectively
We've lost our open strength
We can't relate, discuss, debate
Our common hurts spent

 Does the real me scare you?

THE FORTRESS:

A fortress was built around the castle of my heart
With flowers and streams running far below
As I watch from my tower on a clear, starry night
With animals playing together in the snow
A scene so pure: God's grace and His Hand

A nautical mile and I'm further out to sea
The waves of my past and my future roll as one
In my yacht I am safe from the storms of my life
I close my eyes so I only see the sun
But I wonder: will I ever see the face of His Land?

A father's eyes lit up as he smiled
As he reached out to take his son in his arms
The beauty of life is the same now as then
So why does the love often become harm
It's the cycle of hurting only God understands

As I sit here in fear wondering what is next
It seems as if God speaks to my heart
He says I must just go on being me
For He knew His plan for my life from the start
My feet can walk sure for my steps are all planned

I realised one day that the fortress isn't real
For my God had been there all along and I never knew
Just how much He had done and how far I had come
He said to me: my child, this is you
I love you, I won't leave you, so be the best that you can.

THE KNIFE:

Once I thought of times gone by
As places, pictures, faces
Now it's changed and though I try
The steps my mind replaces

Empty hearts, nothing fills
To me the circle means:
Trusted promise, blood spills
Over hurtful, wasted scenes

As much as I have loved and dared
To give my heart, love, life
Returning, broken and prepared
To lift the power, graded, knife

Against me, into, through my soul
It cuts to deeper hurt
Dividing, tearing, what once was whole
The knife: rejection's revert.

THE LOSS OF YOU:

The ache of longing returned anew
Drawing bittersweet memories of you

* You completed me, you lifted my soul
   You made what once was broken whole
   You gave me joy and courage to hope
   You were my strength when I couldn't cope

* My whole life and all I am
   Once held safely in your hands
   So much shared, so much lost
   Never did I dream of such a cost

The loss of you cuts worse than a knife
Give me death rather than this life.

THE RIVER:

When at first we met I thought
I cannot allow another near
It took two weeks working through the hurt
Confusing, sometimes times of fear
Thought not without extreme faith and love
I saw you here and always enough

Growing responsibility
For you, and you, and you; me
If you knew this mind I seek
You'd turn, hurt, once retreat

Taught, stretched, an elastic band
My mind, far beyond capacity
Or so it seems. Task in hand
Fighting it for liberty

I wandered by a river
On my way home today
And saw the life of flowing
Past the present, its own way

And me I'm left here
And long to have you near
You'd be disappointed if you knew the river flows
Away from me, away from here, without me

The river goes.

THE ROSE:

Like a rose-bud opens: bit by bit
Slowly, wondrously drawn
So my heart is tentative. Revealing it
Painfully faces dawn

A deep rich red people stop to see
A heavenly loving heart
This pleasure to behold: the rose or me?
Either way growth starts

Where does it come from? People ask
This heavenly living scent?
The me in the rose in me behind glass
From a broken stem sent.

THE SHADOW OF ME:

Take me away from this world I despise
For I am the cause of my true love's demise
Whenever I'm near I see someone fall
The dance of my life 'till curtain's call

But once in your life comes a different light
No matter how close it still burns bright
If this is the same as all the times before
Sometime soon you'll be out that door

Chances taken become chances lost
Paying the price means counting the cost
Holding another's heart in mine
Eternity's captured in this moment in time

Rivers of life pass me by
Everyday, every time I have to ask why
For whenever my heart joins another in flight
The turn of the tide washes in the night

  * And I see you here as I watch beyond the shadow of me
    I want you near but the chance has gone for this life to be

THE TENANT:

Again the familiar; the safe
Or is it?

You: and your words remain
The tenant

Always present; can't complain
I started

My pain, sensitivity
Just an extension of me

You yourself, unaware
Of what's left there

I'm left, thwarted
Attempts, love, aborted.

THE TRUTH:

My heart was torn at once between
Passions, responsibilities
Your loyalty evident to see
Disappointed though you seemed

Do we not feel the same
Or is this love's foolish game
My feelings, hurts, to you so plain
Retracted, told to refrain

Joyous love, a new-found thing
Ecstatic, flowing, turbulent spring
My love, my life, myself I bring
In essence always everything

I know it's there, you feel it too
Between us then, now, it's true
Is it me, alone, forever doomed
Without the loving arms of you

Or will you accept the truth?

THE WAY:

From an ancient creed
Comes a powerful seed
Be the one who knows

More passion inside
The heart's reply
Endless, aching flow

How can I be
The real me
Sunken, deep below

A glorious strength
A sunshine
A new day
Returns, the way to show.

TRAPPED:

Division of mind from body, as floating on air. Juxtaposed mind and will - cannot exist together; yet do. A fuzzy veil hangs before me, and my eyes illuminate only that which is immediately before me, and only after they are blinked repeatedly. I cannot focus, think, concentrate, stay awake, function. Weighted down, I'm drowning in air. I ask questions, but I cannot hear myself. Again the river takes me, washes me away from myself, life, sanity. I wonder at the extension of myself. How am I with-out myself, standing outside, back, watching myself?

I test myself and the world. How far can one push oneself? And what does "out of your mind" mean anyway? How does one know?

Food has become a repulsion; alcohol a craving. I can't stop sleeping, and even when I'm awake I'm busy sleeping. The harshness of focusing dissipates concentration; and words, meanings, explanations escape my understanding. I long to be physically sick, so I can curl up and retreat from the world of tired explanations, into one of childlike dependence and happiness.

I see myself as an excess of what I was, what I should be. Though the scale should reassure of fluctuation within my standard boundaries, I cannot somehow see it that way.

Before my eyes flash constantly the images of a faulty me. Before subconscious, now real on the inside of my eyelids. The movie of wrong choices, mistakes, failures plays before me, inside me, within me.

I shake my head; nothing. Emptiness fills me. Every muscle in my body aches.

I reach out for help.
Nothing moves.
I cannot move.
Trapped.

I know I am here; yet who is here? I'm not sure I even know who I am. Trying to climb out, the walls sinking-sand beneath me; whilst landslides perpetuate downward mobility.

Trapped.

Forever is a long time; or it ends right here.
Night-time should come; envelope me, draw me within itself. A wilted flower.

Time ticks backwards as I will my hand to lift. The only thing I can make myself do is write.

The only thing I want to do is cry. Cry until the well runs dry. Cry until someone stops.

Nothing is my anchor. Listless I flap in the wind. Like an old discarded newspaper, I brush against the legs of fellow man. I look up, desperate.

Shaken off quickly.

I land between feet. Trampled. Somewhere between hell and me there is life.
Life. Somewhere.

Trapped.

WAITING AT HOME:

You were there from the start
You watched as God enveloped my heart
We shared the beginning of my life
Hearts knelt in God's glorious Light

You guided me from that very first day
Mentor and child in every way
Little did I realise what my life would become
Weighted and heavy, an added sum

Without our God, life is ended
Mortals hopeless frailty rendered
For God the only Light in darkness burns
Forever a desperate, dark heart yearns

I didn't know how far I'd gone
Until you showed me what was wrong
The plant from the vine removed
Its lifeblood dry, death ensued

My life I owe to my Saviour's heart
His mercy from me ne'er depart
But without you, my friend, I'd be
Left in the dark for eternity

  * Always remember wherever you roam
    A heart that loves you waits at home.

WAR OF LIFE:

Fears of life entwine my day
Brought to pass somehow, some way
Forever afraid, forever enchained
Mask my face, my cries, my pain
Hide my thoughts and carry this weight
The war of life seals my fate.

WHEN LOVE AWOKE:

Your love today reached across the years
Your voice, your smile, wiped away my tears
You lifted me up from the depths of my hell
To a shining place where hope can dwell

In the light of your eyes were a million words
In the touch of your hand, a lifetime stirred
When the weight of my pain you willingly chose to bear
I broke inside at a heart that cares

* You restored my faith and you gave me hope
  My life was changed the day love awoke.

WITHDRAWAL:

Weigh me down, this longing knife
Pierce my heart and destroy this life
Blinding pain somehow draws me too
Glass that cuts when I can't see you

I need to be near enough to feel
Only your touch enough to heal
Yet time away cuts worse than glass
Only you can make this pain pass

To love more than love's allowed
Burn with longing to be near somehow
Desperate to be with you, I ache with loss
Withdrawal from you, my sin's cost.

YEARNING:

I love you more than life itself
What would you do if you knew
Would you run away
Or care enough to stay
And allow me to hold onto you

I want to be by your side
Always close to your heart
But how could it be
When you don't love me
And my love drives us apart

Is this how it will always be
Hearts bound in stone
My love unreturned
In my soul burns
And my heart yearns alone.

YELLOW ROSE:

Memories flooded me
I looked upon a rose
Yellow, almost hauntingly
As another chapter closed

The first bud pushing
A peaceful humility
Growth from within
Granted serenity

Time and circumstances
Shape and weather
Young beauty; chances
A journey towards forever

Tender love draws open truth
Fortified strength anew
Love, compassion, grounded youth
An eternal, magnificent view

The past behind, the future before
Yellow is the colour of your open door

Walk through it to your repose
Today all see and all know
The strength of you
A yellow rose.

YOU:

The birds are singing but I don't hear them call
It's raining outside but I don't see drops fall
The grass is green and the trees are too
But I see none of this
I only see you

YOUR EMBRACE:

When my heart is touched by another's pain
Emotion wells inside again
And tears run free down both my cheeks
My voice too choked inside to speak

Gently you always seem to know
What pain my face masks below
Even when we're far apart
You always know what's in my heart

I think of you and long to be
Against your chest, your arms around me
Tenderly held and powerfully safe
No better place than your embrace

YOUR STRENGTH:

For ages past
Angels tread
On the spur of the moment
A life's dread
One to one come those in pain
Drawn to your strength
Time and again

www.ingramcontent.com/pod-product-compliance
Lightning Source LLC
Chambersburg PA
CBHW020513100426
42813CB00030B/3224/J